06

962

c98

JAPANESE COOKING

Compiled by Judith Ferguson
Tested and Prepared by Jacqueline Bellefontaine

1564
This edition published in 1991 by Tiger Books International PLC, London
© 1987 Coombe Books
Printed and bound in Singapore
All rights reserved
ISBN 1 85501 119 0

JAPANESE COOKING

TIGER BOOKS INTERNATIONAL
LONDON

CONTENTS

The words simplicity and elegance define Japanese cooking best. With no complicated sauces to distract from the main ingredients, Japanese cooking calls for a few perfect ingredients, exquisitely prepared. Garnishes are kept to a minimum, but they are like miniature sculptures. The Japanese love of pure ingredients stems from the people's love and reverence for nature and all that comes from it. Often, food is garnished with leaves, pine needles or sea plants to remind each person of its origins. Study the artistic arrangement of a Japanese dish and you will see the roots of nouvelle cuisine.

The chapters in this book follow the order of courses at a formal Japanese banquet. Each of the following courses illustrates an important technique in Japanese cooking:

1 Zensai – hors d'oeuvres
2 Sumashi-jiru – clear soups (we have combined this course with miso soups, which normally appear later in the meal)
3 Sashimi – raw fish and garnishes
4 Yakimono – grilled/broiled and pan-fried food
5 Mushimono – steamed and baked food
6 Nimono – simmered food
7 Agemono – deep-fried food (Nabemono, one pot dishes such as Sukiyaki, are included in the chapter on simmered food, and sometimes take the place of courses 4-7)

8 Sunomo or Aemono – vinegared food and salads
9 Gohan – rice
10 Miso-shiru – miso soups
11 Tsukemono – pickles
12 Green tea
13 Fresh fruit or desserts

If the number of courses seems daunting, remember that each course is a small serving by Western standards, and that two or three courses can make an excellent meal on their own. Also, don't imagine that you need a vast kitchen filled with specialised equipment – average kitchens in Japan are small, with very basic appliances – everyday kitchen utensils are quite adequate, and sharp knives are an absolute must. Woks are not traditional Japanese cookware, but they adapt well for steaming or frying. Ingredients do not have to be unusual, merely as fresh and good looking as possible, to maintain the Japanese standard. It is, however, useful to have a basic understanding of the following Japanese ingredients:

Adzuki beans – Small dried red beans. Used in rice dishes and sweets.
Agar-agar – Vegetable gelatine sold in blocks or powder. Needs soaking in liquid before use. Use normal gelatine.
Bamboo shoots – First shoots of the bamboo plant. Fresh shoots are best, but the canned variety is more readily available. Rinse canned shoots before use.

Bonito flakes, dried – Used to make dashi, the basic stock for soups and simmering. Also sprinkled on food to garnish. Sold pre-packaged, the flakes are made from fillets of a mackerel-like fish.

Daikon – A large, white radish, used cooked or raw. Often used grated as a garnish or ingredient in a dipping sauce. Do not substitute pink or red radishes.

Ginger – Knobbly root with a spicy, hot taste. Peel and grate for use. Pickled ginger is often used as a garnish, grated or sliced, for grilled/broiled meats. Red or pink in its pickled form.

Glutinous rice – A round-grain variety which cooks to a sticky consistency essential for sushi or vinegared-rice dishes and for picking up with chopsticks. Short-grain rice can be substituted. Rice is so important in Japanese cooking that it is used as a course in itself. For plain boiled rice use long-grain or Patna rice.

Kamaboko – Fish paste sold in a rectangular cake, tinted pink or light green with a white centre.

Konbu – A greenish-brown kelp and an important flavouring in dashi. Sold dried, it should be stored tightly covered.

Konnyaku – Gelatinous vegetable paste formed into a cake. It absorbs tastes and colours of foods it is cooked with. Stored in water, it will keep for up to two weeks if the water is changed every day.

Lotus root – Root of the waterlily. Cross-section slice looks like a flower. Available fresh or canned from Japanese groceries.

Mirin – Fermented soy bean paste. Used as a soup base, condiment, sauce ingredient or salad dressing. It comes in a light or white variety, or dark, reddish colour. A yellow variety is the most common.

Noodles – Harusame are transparent noodles made from rice. Shirataki noodles are made from devil's tongue root. Both are often called cellophane noodles. Soba are buckwheat noodles. Udon are white noodles made from wheat flour and vary in length and thickness. Somen noodles are the thinnest. Both buckwheat and udon noodles are available dried or fresh in vacuum-sealed packs.

Nori – Laver (seaweed) used to wrap sushi, or shredded to use as a garnish. Sold in thin sheets.

Sesame seeds – Both black and white varieties are used.

Seven-taste (or spice) pepper – A combination of red pepper, sanso pepper, ground orange peel, sesame seed, hemp seed, poppy seed and ground nori seaweed. Usually used to season food at the table.

Shiitake mushroom – Available fresh or dried, the latter being the more common form. Dried mushrooms must be soaked in water for 30 minutes before use, and the stems are removed before cooking.

Shiso leaves – Bright green leaves from a small herb plant. Used as a garnish and available fresh from Japanese groceries. They have a mint-like flavour.

Soy sauce – Japanese type is lighter and sweeter than Chinese. Light variety is saltier than the dark.

Tofu – White cake made from soy bean curd, and custard-like in texture. Usually sold in water-packed cartons, it needs to be thoroughly drained before use. Can be stored in the refrigerator if kept in water that is changed daily.

Trefoil – A herb related to parsley. Use salad cress as a substitute.

Vinegar – Made from rice and pale yellow in colour.

Wasabi horseradish – Pale green powdered root with a very hot, pungent taste. Mix with water to a smooth paste and shape into mounds or small leaf shapes. Use as an accompaniment to sashimi or an addition to dipping sauce.

Japanese garnishes are beautiful and, with practice, not difficult to make. The following are the easiest and the ones used in these recipes:

Carrot spurs – Cut a carrot into 7.5cm/3 inch sections and peel. Place in boiling water for about 4 minutes. Carve lengthwise with a sharp knife or dannelle knife. Cut triangular grooves down the length of each carrot. Cut crosswise into slices.

Carrot twists – Cut carrot into 7.5cm/3 inch sections and peel. Slice thinly, lengthwise. Make a 2.5cm/1 inch slit in the centre of each slice. Soak the pieces in salt water for at least 10 minutes. Rinse. When pieces are pliable, slip one end of each piece through the slit in the middle and pull back.

Carrot blossoms – Cut carrot in 7.5cm/3 inch sections. Slice five sides to form a pentagon. with a knife or cannelle knife make five lengthwise triangular cuts on all five sides. Trim the top of the carrot so that one end is higher than the other. Slice the flowers thinly, turning as you slice. Go around twice to make double flowers.

Cucumber twigs – Cut 5cm/2 inch sections from an unpeeled cucmber. Slice one side lengthwise off this section, about 6mm/¼ inch thick. Cut a centre section from this piece about 5cm/2 inches wide. In this section, make two lengthwise cuts from either end. Do not cut all the way through. Each cut should end 6cm/¼ inch from the opposite end. Twist the two outer strips so that they cross over. The same thing can be done with a thick piece of lemon rind.

Courgette/zucchini fan or comet – cut the ends off. Slice in half, lengthwise. Make a series of cuts, close together down the length of one half, leaving a spine along the side to hold the slices together. Soak in salt water for at least 10 minutes. Rinse. Spread out on a serving plate. Add a carrot spur.

Radish flowers – Cut stems and tips from radishes. Make two cuts in each of the four sides. Tip should be uppermost. Cut a cross in the top. Soak in ice water until the slice opens.

Radish fans – Choose radishes with leaves. Cut the tip off the radish and cut lengthwise, but not quite through to the leaf end. Soak in salt water and spread out on a plate.

Radish jacks – Slice a radish into thin rounds, Cut a notch in each slice. Slide one slice into the notch of the other.

Lemon and cucumber whirls – Thinly slice lemons and cucumbers. Notch each slice and twist.

Scored mushrooms – Soak dried shiitake mushrooms in hot water for 30 minutes. Cut off the stems and make a cross in the middle of the top of each cap.

JAPANESE COOKING

HORS D'OEUVRES

Lemon-Ikura

PREPARATION TIME: 5 minutes

SERVES: 4 people

20g/4 rounded tsps salmon roe (large grain)
4 thin slices lemon
2 chives, very finely shredded

Arrange the lemon slices on a serving dish. Mound a spoonful of roe on top of each slice. Garnish each with a few shreds of chive. Serve cold as part of a selection of hors d'oeuvres.

Fresh Vegetables with Sauces

PREPARATION TIME: 30 minutes

COOKING TIME: 2 minutes

SERVES: 4 people

Selection of the following:
Mangetout/pea pods (2 per person, stems trimmed)
Courgettes/zucchini (if small, 1 per person, sliced in half. If large, cut 1 into thin strips)
Carrots (as for courgettes/zucchini)
French/green beans (2 per person, stems trimmed)
Shiitake mushrooms, dried (1 per person, cut in quarters if large)
Daikon radish (as for carrots)
Turnips (1 large or 2 small, peeled, quartered and sliced)
Leeks (1 small thin one cut into 2.5cm/ 1 inch pieces)

SOY AND LEMON SAUCE
90ml/6 tbsps soy sauce
60ml/4 tbsps fresh lemon juice

SESAME SAUCE
45ml/3 tbsps white sesame seeds

30ml/2 tbsps mirin
90ml/6 tbsps soy sauce
60ml/4 tbsps dashi

Fresh Vegetables with Sauces.

Place the vegetables in a steamer or on a rack above boiling water. Cover well and cook 2 minutes. Mix the ingredients for each sauce and divide the mixture among 8 small bowls. Arrange the vegetables attractively on 4 serving plates and serve with the dipping sauces.

Prawns/Shrimp in Nori Packages

PREPARATION TIME: 20 minutes

COOKING TIME: 2 minutes

SERVES: 4 people

This page: Lemon-Ikura. Facing page: Pink, White and Green Rolls (top) and Prawns/Shrimp in Nori Packages (bottom).

4 king prawns/jumbo shrimp
1 square nori
4 chives

GRILLING SAUCE
30ml/2 tbsps soy sauce
15ml/1 tbsp mirin
15ml/1 tbsp grated ginger squeezed for
   juice

GARNISH
Courgette/zucchini fan (see introduction)

Shell and de-vein the prawns/shrimp, but leave on the tail ends. Pass the sheet of nori over a gas flame on both sides to freshen it. Cut it into 4 strips. Mix all the sauce ingredients together and brush the prawns/shrimp. Brush the nori strips and wrap one around each prawn/shrimp, but do not completely cover. Place under a pre-heated grill/broiler and cook for 1 minute on each side, brushing with the remaining sauce. Tie each with 1 chive. If desired, prepare double quantity sauce and use some for dipping. Garnish with prepared courgette/zucchini fan.

Tofu-Dengaku

PREPARATION TIME: 20 minutes
COOKING TIME: 5-6 minutes
SERVES: 4 people

90g/3oz tofu, well drained, pressed for
   15 minutes and sliced into rectangles
   5cm/2 inches long and 1.25cm/½ inch
   thick
25g/1½ tbsps miso
25ml/1½ tbsps mirin
25ml/1½ tbsps dashi
15g/½ oz spinach, cooked and puréed or
   defrosted and well drained
15g/1 tbsp white sesame seeds

GARNISH
Radish flower (see introduction)

Prepare the garnish. Place the tofu in a steamer or on a rack above boiling water. Cover and cook for 5-6 minutes. Combine the remaining ingredients, except spinach and sesame seeds, in a small pan and cook slowly until very thick. Add the

spinach and mix well. Place tofu on serving dishes and insert small bamboo skewers lengthwise. Spread the spinach mixture evenly over each piece of tofu and sprinkle with sesame seeds. Garnish with radish flower.

Chicken Livers with Cucumber

PREPARATION TIME: 25 minutes
COOKING TIME: 5-6 minutes
SERVES: 4-6 people

15ml/1 tbsp oil
180g/6oz chicken livers, picked over and
   trimmed
10ml/2 tsps grated ginger, squeezed for
   juice
10ml/2 tsps mirin
10ml/2 tsps soy sauce
½ cucumber, peeled in stripes
15ml/1 tbsp white sesame seeds

Heat the oil in a frying pan. Cut the chicken livers into even-sized pieces, but not too small. Put into the hot oil and cook over high heat, turning frequently to brown on the outside. Pour in the soy sauce, mirin and ginger juice and continue to cook 1-2 minutes over medium heat. Livers may be served slightly pink inside. Toss half the livers with sesame seeds to coat. Cut the cucumber half in quarters, lengthwise, and then into pieces the size of the livers. Thread one sesame-seed-coated liver, one piece of cucumber and one plain liver onto small bamboo skewers to serve.

Pink, White and Green Rolls

PREPARATION TIME: 30 minutes,
plus chilling time
COOKING TIME: 2 minutes
SERVES: 8 people

8cm/3 inch piece of daikon (white)
   radish, peeled
8 large or 16 small spinach leaves
120g/4oz smoked salmon, thinly sliced
Pinch salt

45ml/3 tbsps rice vinegar
45g/3 tbsps sugar

Trim the piece of daikon radish into a large cube. Cut the cube into 16 very thin slices. Soak in 570ml/1 pint/2 cups water with 10ml/2 tsps salt for about 20 minutes to soften. Wash spinach leaves well and remove thick stalks. Cook 2 minutes in a covered saucepan with a pinch of salt until just wilted. Rinse in cold water and pat dry. Place the salmon slices in 4 rows. Place the spinach leaves, evenly divided, on top of the salmon. Divide the radish slices evenly among the four rows and place on top of the spinach. Roll up and secure with cocktail sticks/wooden picks. Mix the vinegar and sugar and pour over the rolls. Refrigerate for 2-3 hours, turning once or twice. When ready to serve, remove the sticks/picks and slice each roll in half, crosswise. Serve cut side up so that a spiral of pink, white and green shows.

Beef and Scallion Rolls

PREPARATION TIME: 25 minutes
COOKING TIME: 12-15 minutes
SERVES: 4 people

4-6 spring/green onions, trimmed and cut
   into 5cm/2 inch lengths
120g/4oz sirloin, fat trimmed, sliced very
   thin and cut into 12 x 5cm/5 x 2 inch
   pieces
15ml/1 tbsp oil
30ml/2 tbsps soy sauce
15ml/1 tbsp sugar
15ml/1 tbsp saké
15ml/1 tbsp dashi
15ml/1 tbsp mirin

GARNISH
Carrot blossoms (see introduction)
Cucumber twigs (see introduction)

Prepare the garnishes. Divide onions equally into 4-6 groups. Roll 1 slice of beef around 1 group of onions. Tie

**Facing page: Tofu-Dengaku (top)
and Chicken Livers with
Cucumber (bottom).**

rolls with string. Repeat with remaining onions and beef. Heat oil in a large heavy-based frying pan. Add the beef rolls, seam side down, and cook about 1 minute over moderate heat. Turn the rolls several times to brown evenly. Reduce the heat and add all remaining

ingredients except the mirin. Cook a further 3 minutes and remove the meat with a slotted spoon. Turn up the heat and cook the pan juices to reduce by half. Add the mirin. Remove the string from the rolls and return them to the pan. Cook the rolls, turning them often, until well

This page: Beef and Scallion Rolls.

glazed. Cut each roll into 1.25cm/ ½ inch thick rounds. Thread the rounds on skewers and garnish.

SOUPS

Summer Chilled Miso Soup

PREPARATION TIME: 25 minutes plus chilling time

COOKING TIME: 25 minutes – 1 hour

SERVES: 4 people

1150ml/2 pints/4 cups chicken stock or dashi
90g/3oz miso
½ small cucumber, thinly sliced
1-2 tomatoes, skinned and sliced
15g/½ oz trefoil (salad cress)

Make the stock as for Sumashi Jiru or dashi as for Butaniku no Dango. Chill thoroughly. Cream the miso with about 280ml/½ pint/1 cup of the stock and add to the remaining stock with all the remaining ingredients.

Butaniku no Dango

PREPARATION TIME: 20 minutes

COOKING TIME: 15 minutes

SERVES: 4 people

DASHI
1.7 litres/3 pints/6 cups water
15g/½ oz konbu seaweed
15g/½ oz shaved, dried bonito fillet

225g/8oz minced/ground pork
2.5ml/½ tsp ground ginger
30ml/2 tbsps soy sauce
15g/½ oz somen noodles
4 spring/green onions shredded

This page: **Sumashi Jiru (Basic Clear Soup) (top)** and **Butaniku no Dango (bottom).**

Bring the water to the boil in a heavy-based pan, add the seaweed and simmer gently 1-2 minutes. Remove the seaweed and add the bonito flakes. Bring back to the boil and then remove from the heat. Allow the bonito flakes to sink to the bottom of the pan and then strain the stock through muslin/ cheesecloth, or a very fine meshed strainer. Combine the pork and ginger and form into small balls. Return the stock to the rinsed-out pan. Add the soy sauce and bring the stock back to the boil. Add the pork balls, cover and simmer gently for 5 minutes. Add the noodles and continue simmering for 5 minutes, until the meat balls and noodles are cooked. Add the spring/green onions and serve.

This page: Summer Chilled Miso Soup. Facing page: Soup with Fish Dumplings (top) and Prawn/ Shrimp Noodle Soup (bottom).

Prawn/Shrimp Noodle Soup

PREPARATION TIME: 20 minutes

COOKING TIME: 25-35 minutes

SERVES: 4 people

STOCK
225g/8oz fish trimmings (head, bones and skin)
1 small onion, studded with 6 cloves
1 small piece ginger root
1.3 litres/2½ pints/5 cups water

SOUP
Strained stock
30g/1oz soba noodles
225g/8oz cooked, peeled prawns/shrimp

GARNISH
Parsley sprigs

Place all the stock ingredients into a heavy-based pan. Bring to the boil and simmer gently for 20-25 minutes. Do not over-boil or stock will taste bitter. Remove scum from the surface and strain through muslin/cheesecloth, or a fine-meshed strainer. Return the stock to the rinsed-out pan. Add the noodles and simmer for 5-10 minutes until noodles are cooked. Add the prawns/shrimp to the hot soup and pour into individual dishes to serve. Garnish with small sprigs of parsley.

Vegetable Miso Soup

PREPARATION TIME: 30 minutes

COOKING TIME: 25 minutes – 1 hour

SERVES: 4 people

1150ml/2 pints/4 cups dashi or chicken stock
30ml/2 tbsps oil
120g/4oz daikon radish, cut into matchsticks
2 carrots, peeled and cut into matchsticks
1 small onion, diced
4 whole okra, stems removed and cut into rounds
4 dried mushrooms, soaked 30 minutes, stalks removed
120g/4oz miso

Make stock as for Sumashi Jiru or dashi as for Butaniku no Dango. Heat oil in a heavy-based pan and sauté radish, carrot and onion. When soft, add the okra, mushrooms, with caps scored if desired, and stock or dashi. Bring almost to the boil and mix about 280ml/½ pint/1 cup of the hot stock with the miso. Add this slowly back to the soup. Remove from heat and serve.

Sumashi Jiru (Basic Clear Soup)

PREPARATION TIME: 20 minutes

COOKING TIME: 55 minutes – 1 hour 10 minutes

SERVES: 4 people

STOCK
1 chicken carcass or about 450g/1lb chicken trimmings (bones, giblets, skin etc.)
1 carrot, peeled and roughly chopped
1 small onion, peeled and roughly chopped
2 sticks celery
1150ml/2 pints/4 cups water

SOUP
Stock (as above), strained
15ml/1 tbsp sherry
30ml/2 tbsps soy sauce
120g/4oz diced, cooked chicken
1 medium carrot
4 sprigs watercress

Break the chicken bones into small pieces and add with the remaining stock ingredients to a heavy-based pan. Bring to the boil and then simmer gently for 45 minutes to 1 hour, occasionally skimming off fat if necessary. Strain through muslin/cheesecloth, or a very fine meshed strainer. Return to the rinsed out pan. Peel the carrot for the soup and pare off small strips with a cannelle knife, or small paring knife, down the length of the carrot. Cut the carrot into slices to form "flowers". Bring the stock to the boil and add the sherry and soy sauce. Season with salt and pepper, if necessary. Add the carrot flowers and chicken and cook gently for 5-10 minutes until the chicken is hot and carrot is just tender. Pour into individual bowls and garnish with watercress.

Miso Soup with Prawns/Shrimp and Fried Tofu

PREPARATION TIME: 25 minutes

COOKING TIME: 25 minutes – 1 hour

SERVES: 4 people

1150ml/2 pints/4 cups chicken stock or dashi
30ml/2 tbsps oil
120g/4oz tofu, drained and cubed
60g/4 tbsps miso
120g/4oz prawns/shrimp
2 spring/green onions, sliced diagonally

GARNISH
4 unshelled prawns/shrimp

Make stock as for Sumashi Jiru or dashi as for Butaniku no Dango. Heat the oil in a frying pan and fry the tofu 2 minutes. Remove from the pan and pour over boiling water to remove excess oil. Drain. Heat most of the stock or dashi in a heavy-based pan until just boiling. Remove from the heat. Mix the remaining stock or dashi with miso and add gradually to the pan. Add the tofu and prawns/shrimp and garnish with sliced spring/green onion and whole prawns/shrimp.

Soup with Fish Dumplings

PREPARATION TIME: 25 minutes

COOKING TIME: 25-35 minutes

SERVES: 4 people

STOCK
340-450g/12oz-1lb whole whitefish (to give 120g/4oz fillets)
1 small onion, studded with 6 cloves
1 small piece ginger root
1.3 litres/2½ pints/5 cups water

Facing page: Miso Soup with Prawns/Shrimp and Fried Tofu (top) and Vegetable Miso Soup (bottom).

1.25ml/¼ tsp ground ginger
2 spring/green onions
1 egg white
60-75ml/4-5 tbsps (approx) plain/
   all-purpose flour
30ml/2 tbsps oil
4 spears asparagus cut diagonally into
   1 inch pieces
Salt and pepper
Rind and juice of 1 lemon
15ml/1 tbsp soy sauce

Fillet and skin the fish, using the trimmings to make stock as for Prawn Noodle Soup. Mince the fish fillets in a food processor with the ground ginger, spring/green onions, egg white, salt and pepper. Gradually blend in flour until mixture is stiff enough to shape into small balls. The mixture will be sticky. Heat the oil in a heavy-based pan and sauté the asparagus until just tender. Add the stock and return to the boil gently. Carefully add the fish dumplings, lemon rind and juice and soy sauce, and simmer for 5-10 minutes until cooked. Serve immediately.

Clear Tofu Soup

PREPARATION TIME: 20 minutes

COOKING TIME: 55 minutes – 1 hour

SERVES: 4 people

1150ml/2 pints/4 cups chicken stock or
   dashi
45ml/3 tbsps soy sauce

This page: Clear Tofu Soup. Facing page: Salmon or Tuna Sashimi.

120g/4oz tofu, drained and cubed
2 small leeks, washed, trimmed and sliced
60g/2oz bean sprouts

Make up stock as for Sumashi Jiru (Basic Clear Soup) or dashi as for Butaniku no Dango. Bring to the boil in a heavy-based pan and add soy sauce and leek slices. Simmer until leeks are tender. Divide between individual dishes and add the tofu and bean sprouts to the hot soup. Serve immediately.

RAW FISH

Tuna Sashimi

PREPARATION TIME: 50 minutes

SERVES: 4 people

225g/8oz tuna fillet
120ml/4 fl oz/½ cup light soy sauce

GARNISH
Carrot twists (see introduction)
Cellophane noodles

Prepare the carrot twists. Skin the fillets and treat as in Salmon Sashimi. Slice the tuna across the grain. Place in shallow serving bowls. Cover cellophane noodles with hot water and soak for 5 minutes. Drain and leave to cool. Arrange carrot twists and a portion of cellophane noodles next to the tuna on each plate.

Salmon or Tuna Sashimi

PREPARATION TIME: 50 minutes

SERVES: 4 people

225g/8oz raw salmon or tuna fillet
½ daikon radish, finely grated

SAUCE
90ml/6 tbsps soy sauce
45ml/3 tbsps lemon juice

GARNISH
4 courgette/zucchini fans (see introduction)
4 carrot spurs (see introduction)

Skin the fish fillet, place in a colander and pour over boiling water. This will not cook the fish. Place immediately into ice-cold water. Pat the fish dry and slice across the grain into 1cm/⅜ inch thick strips. Arrange daikon radish in mounds in 4 serving bowls. Place the slices of fish against the daikon radish mounds. Mix the soy sauce and lemon juice and divide into 4 small bowls. Garnish with prepared courgette/zucchini fans and carrot spurs arranged to look like a comet.

Scallop Sashimi

PREPARATION TIME: 50 minutes

SERVES: 4 people

4 large or 8 small, fresh scallops with roe, if possible
4 shiso leaves
4 lemon twigs (see introduction)
30g/2 tbsps wasabi horseradish powder mixed with water to a thick paste

SAUCE
90ml/6 tbsps light soy sauce
30ml/2 tbsps lemon juice

Wash the scallops in cold, salted water. Pat dry and slice into very thin rounds, leaving the roe in one piece. Overlap slices of scallops in serving dish or place roe on one side. Decorate with shiso leaves and lemon twigs. Mix the soy sauce and lemon juice together and serve one bowl of the sauce with each serving of sashimi.

Squid Sashimi

PREPARATION TIME: 50 minutes

SERVES: 4 people

1 squid (prepared squid are available from fishmongers and Japanese markets)
1 carrot, finely grated

SAUCE
120ml/4 fl oz/½ cup soy sauce
Pinch wasabi powder

GARNISH
Fennel or dill fronds
4 radish fans (see introduction)

Prepare the radish fans. Wash the squid in cold, salted water and pat dry. Lightly score one side of the squid and then cut into 1cm/⅜ inch thick strips, crosswise. Place a mound

of carrot on each serving dish. Place the squid against the mound of carrot. Mix the soy sauce and the wasabi and pour into 4 small bowls. Garnish with fennel or dill and prepared radish fans.

This page: Tuna Sashimi. Facing page: Scallop Sashimi (top) and Squid Sashimi (bottom).

JAPANESE COOKING

GRILLING AND PAN-FRYING

Beef and Leek Skewers

PREPARATION TIME: 25 minutes

COOKING TIME: 8-10 minutes

SERVES: 4 people

450g/1lb rump/butt steak, cut in
*   3.75cm/1½ inch cubes*
4 leeks, cut in 3.75cm/1½ inch pieces,
*   white and pale green part only*
45ml/3 tbsps oil
60g/4 tbsps sugar
30ml/2 tbsps mirin
15ml/1 tbsp grated ginger
120ml/4 fl oz/½ cup soy sauce
Pinch black pepper

GARNISH
Lemon slices

Thread the leeks and beef alternately
onto bamboo skewers. This should
fill 2-3 skewers per person. Pour oil
into a large frying pan. When hot,
add 2 skewers at a time and brown all
sides well, about 1-2 minutes. Drain
off any excess oil and mix the
remaining ingredients. Pour over the
meat and cook a further 2-3 minutes.
Remove the meat and simmer until
the sauce is thick and syrupy, about
5 minutes. Pour over the meat and
garnish with lemon slices.

Chicken Yakitori

PREPARATION TIME: 30 minutes

COOKING TIME: 5-6 minutes

SERVES: 4 people

60ml/4 tbsps mirin
60ml/4 tbsps sake
140ml/¼ pint/½ cup soy sauce

Pinch cayenne pepper
1 clove garlic
1 small piece ginger
5ml/1 tsp sugar

**This page: Chicken Yakitori. Facing
page: Pork Kebabs with Vegetables
(top) and Beef and Leek Skewers
(bottom).**

1 chicken, skinned, boned and cut in
   2.5cm/1 inch pieces
2 large green peppers, cored, seeded and
   cut in 2.5cm/1 inch pieces
2-4 leeks, depending on size (substitute
   spring/green onions when leeks are out
   of season)

GARNISH
Radish jacks (see introduction)

Combine the first 7 ingredients in a
small pan and bring to the boil.
Remove from the heat and set aside
to cool. Pour over the chicken and
marinate for 30 minutes. Wash the
leeks well and cut off the dark green
tops. Cut the white and pale green
parts into 2.5cm/1 inch pieces. If the
leeks are very thick, cut in half.
Thread 2 pieces of chicken onto
bamboo or metal skewers, followed
by a piece of pepper and leek until all
the ingredients are used. This will
make 2-3 skewers per person.
Reserve the marinade. Pre-heat a
grill/broiler and cook the chicken
skewers 5-6 minutes per side, basting
frequently with the marinade. May be
cooked on a charcoal grill as well.
Garnish with radish jacks.

Pork Kebabs with Vegetables

PREPARATION TIME: 30 minutes

COOKING TIME: 5-6 minutes

SERVES: 4 people

1 small aubergine/eggplant
2 green peppers
1 onion, cut in 2.5cm/1 inch pieces
340g/12oz pork fillet/tenderloin

SAUCE
30ml/2 tbsps oil
30ml/2 tbsps soy sauce
45ml/3 tbsps Worcestershire sauce
45ml/3 tbsps ketchup
15ml/1 tbsp grated ginger, squeezed for
   juice
1 clove garlic, finely minced

GARNISH
Lemon and cucumber twists (see
   introduction)

Slice the aubergine/eggplant in half
and score lightly. Sprinkle with salt
and leave to stand 30 minutes. Cut
the peppers in half and remove seeds.
Cut into 2.5cm/1 inch pieces. Cut
the pork into 2.5cm/1 inch pieces.
Squeeze the juices from the
aubergine/eggplant and rinse well.
Pat dry and cut into pieces the size of
the pork. Thread the ingredients
onto bamboo or metal skewers,
beginning with pork and alternating
between pork and vegetables, ending
with pork. This should make 2-3
kebabs per person. Mix the sauce
ingredients thoroughly. Brush the
kebabs and place under a pre-heated
grill/broiler. Cook 5-6 minutes,
turning every 2 minutes, until the
pork is cooked. Brush frequently
with the sauce. Serve remaining
sauce in separate bowls. Garnish with
lemon and cucumber twists.

Beef Teriyaki

PREPARATION TIME: 30 minutes

COOKING TIME: 12-14 minutes

SERVES: 4 people

Light cooking oil, such as soya or
   groundnut/peanut oil
1 large onion, sliced
4 very small courgettes/zucchini, ends
   trimmed
8 small or 4 large mushrooms, halved and
   scored
4 rump/butt steaks about 120g/4oz in
   weight

SAUCE
60ml/4 tbsps dark soy sauce
60ml/4 tbsps sake
45ml/3 tbsps mirin
1 clove garlic, finely chopped
1 small piece ginger, finely chopped

Pour about 30ml/2 tbsps oil into a
large frying pan. When hot, place in
the onion slices in one layer. Fry until
golden brown on both sides, about
1-2 minutes. Remove and keep warm.
Cut the courgettes/zucchini into
thin rounds. Add 30ml/2 tbsps more
oil to the pan and cook the
courgettes/zucchini quickly over
high heat. Set aside and add the

mushrooms to the pan. Cook
1 minute and set aside. Keep all the
vegetables warm while cooking the
steaks. Add more oil to the pan and
keep the heat high. Cook 1 steak at a
time until both sides are brown,
about 1 minute per side. Put all the
steaks into the pan, pour over the
sauce and cover. Cook over
moderate heat 1-2 minutes. Divide all
the vegetables evenly among 4 plates.
Place steaks on the plates and cut in
half, lengthwise, then into about 8
short strips. Pour the sauce over the
steaks to serve.

Tuna Teriyaki

PREPARATION TIME: 20 minutes

COOKING TIME: 17 minutes

SERVES: 4 people

4 tuna fish steaks
30ml/2 tbsps oil
60ml/4 tbsps soy sauce
15ml/1 tbsp mirin
15ml/1 tbsp sugar
15ml/1 tbsp miso

GARNISH
Radish flowers and leaves (see
   introduction)

Heat the oil in a large frying pan.
Add the tuna and cook until slightly
browned, about 2 minutes. Drain
away excess oil and add the soy
sauce, mirin and sugar. Cook over
very low heat to cook the fish, about
5 minutes. Remove the fish from the
pan and keep warm. Cook liquid
over high heat to reduce by half. Stir
in the miso. Skin tuna steaks and
separate carefully in half. Discard
bones and skin. Pour sauce over the
fish and garnish with radish flowers
and leaves.

**Facing page: Beef Teriyaki (top)
and Tuna Teriyaki (bottom).**

Grilled/Broiled Green Peppers

PREPARATION TIME: 15 minutes

COOKING TIME: 4-5 minutes

SERVES: 4 people

4 medium-sized green peppers
30ml/2 tbsps oil
Sesame seeds
Pickled ginger

Quarter the peppers and remove the seeds and cores. Heat a grill/broiler and brush the peppers on all sides with oil. Cook for 4-5 minutes, turning the peppers every minute. During the last minute of cooking, turn the peppers skin side up and sprinkle over the sesame seeds. Allow the seeds to brown slightly and then remove the peppers to a serving dish. Serve with grated pickled ginger, if desired.

Flying Fish

PREPARATION TIME: 40 minutes

COOKING TIME: 4-10 minutes

SERVES: 4 people

4 fresh small sea bream, trout or red
*   mullet*
Salt
Soy sauce
GARNISH
4 shiso leaves
4 lemon twigs

Scale the fish and gut them through the gills (a fishmonger will prepare the fish in this way). Rinse the fish very well and pat dry. Place the fish with the heads all pointing to the right and the stomach in front of you. Starting just behind the eye area, thread one or two metal skewers 3 times through 1 side of the fish. Do not allow the skewers to penetrate both sides of the fish. Bend the fish slightly every time the skewers are threaded through. Rub salt into the fins to make them stand up. Coat the tail with salt as well. Make sure the salt coating is quite heavy. Pre-heat a grill/broiler and place the fish on a

rack, the side not penetrated by skewers uppermost. Grill/broil 2-5 minutes per side. Twist the skewers occasionally to make them easier to remove. Place the fish on individual serving plates with the side grilled first uppermost. Remove the skewers and garnish with the shiso leaves and lemon twigs. Serve the soy sauce in individual bowls for dipping.

Egg Roll

PREPARATION TIME: 20 minutes

COOKING TIME: 1-2 minutes

SERVES: 3 people

4 eggs, beaten
90ml/3 fl oz/⅓ cup dashi
Pinch salt
1.25ml/¼ tsp light soy sauce
2 spring/green onions, roughly chopped
1 shiitake mushroom, roughly chopped
1 sheet nori, finely shredded
GARNISH
½ daikon radish, finely grated

This is best made in a special oblong Japanese omelette pan. A large frying pan may be substituted. Mix the eggs with the dashi, salt and soy sauce. Brush the pan with a light film of oil. Heat until slightly smoking. Pour in enough of the egg to coat the bottom of the pan. Cook for a few seconds, until the egg is just set. Sprinkle over the onions and mushroom. Roll up the omelette and push to one side of the pan. Brush the pan again with oil and pour in more of the egg. Cook again until just set. Roll up the first omelette inside the second and repeat until all the egg is used. Lift out of the pan and cut into nine rolls. Pass the nori over a gas flame on both sides to freshen. Shred finely. Arrange nori strips on plates and place 3 rolls on top. Garnish with a little grated daikon radish.

This page: Flying Fish. Facing page: Egg Roll (top) and Grilled/Broiled Green Peppers (bottom).

JAPANESE COOKING

STEAMING AND BAKING

Prawn/Shrimp Egg Custard

PREPARATION TIME: 20 minutes

COOKING TIME: 20-25 minutes

SERVES: 4 people

STOCK
570ml/1 pint/2 cups dashi
5ml/1 tsp soy sauce
5ml/1 tsp mirin
Pinch salt

4 dried shiitake mushrooms, soaked
   30 minutes, drained and scored
4 king prawns/jumbo shrimp
4 mangetout/pea pods, blanched and cut
   in half
30g/1oz bean sprouts
5 eggs, beaten

GARNISH
1 piece pickled ginger, grated

Bring stock ingredients to the boil.
Take off the heat and leave to cool.
Strain the stock and when cool mix
with the beaten eggs. Divide the
mixture evenly among 4 heat-
resistant cups or small bowls. Add
the bean sprouts and position the
prawns/shrimp so the tail shows.
Add the mangetout/pea pods and
float a mushroom on top of the
custard. Pour water into a steamer or
a large, deep saucepan and bring to
the boil. Place the cups on a steamer
or a rack above the boiling water.
Cover the pan or steamer and cook

This page: Prawn/Shrimp Egg
Custard. Facing page: Steamed
Abalone (top) and Baked Stuffed
Trout (bottom).

over high heat for about 2 minutes. Reduce the heat and steam until just set, about 15 minutes. A toothpick inserted into the middle of the custard should come out clean when the custard is cooked. Garnish with the pickled ginger.

Baked Stuffed Trout

PREPARATION TIME: 20 minutes

COOKING TIME: 16-19 minutes

OVEN TEMPERATURE:
400°F/200°C/Gas Mark 6

SERVES: 4 people

4 small trout, cleaned and boned

STUFFING
60g/4 tbsps red miso
2 spring/green onions, chopped
30g/2 tbsps sugar
15ml/1 tbsp mirin
15ml/1 tbsp dashi
15ml/1 tbsp grated ginger

GARNISH
Lime slices

Make sure the heads and tails of the fish are left on. Cut 4 pieces of foil large enough to enclose each fish. Brush lightly with oil. Combine stuffing ingredients in a saucepan. Cook over moderate heat 4 minutes to thicken. Place each fish on a piece of foil and spread the stuffing in the cavity. Fold the foil over the fish tightly and twist the ends. Bake 12-14 minutes. Partially open the foil to serve. Garnish with a slice of lime.

Beef Roasted with Vegetables

PREPARATION TIME: 25 minutes

COOKING TIME: 15 minutes

OVEN TEMPERATURE:
400°F/200°C/Gas Mark 6

SERVES: 4 people

450g/1lb sirloin or rib roast, sliced in very thin strips

8 shiitake mushrooms, quartered lengthwise
1 green pepper, cored, seeded and cut in 8 pieces, lengthwise
1 carrot, quartered
60ml/4 tbsps mirin
60ml/4 tbsps soy sauce
Seven spices pepper

DIPPING SAUCE
60ml/4 tbsps lemon juice
60ml/4 tbsps orange juice
120ml/4 fl oz/½ cup soy sauce
120ml/4 fl oz/½ cup dashi

GARNISH
1 small piece daikon radish
1 small red chili pepper
4 shiso leaves
4 orange slices

Cut 4 pieces of foil about 25cm/ 10 inches square. Brush with oil. Place an equal portion of beef, bamboo shoots, peppers, mushroom and carrot on the foil. Mix mirin, soy sauce and seven spice pepper together and pour over each portion. Wrap well and cook 15 minutes. Combine sauce ingredients and pour into 4 small bowls. Remove core from the radish with a vegetable peeler. Insert chili pepper and grate together, finely. Arrange a leaf on each serving plate. Add grated daikon radish and chili pepper and an orange slice. Open the foil packets and place one on each dish. Serve each person with a sauce bowl for dipping.

Steamed Abalone

PREPARATION TIME: 30 minutes

COOKING TIME: 20 minutes

SERVES: 4 people

4 fresh abalone in the shell, if possible
Salt
60ml/4 tbsps sake

MISO SAUCE
90ml/⅓ cup red miso
60ml/4 tbsps dashi
30ml/2 tbsps sugar
30ml/2 tbsps mirin

GARNISH
4 large pieces konbu seaweed
60g/2oz pickled ginger, sliced

Use a strong spatula to remove the abalone if in the shell. Scrub the shells well and reserve. Sprinkle the abalone liberally with salt and scrub to remove black portion. Peel off green edges with a knife. Lightly score the surface of the abalone and line the shells or serving dishes with the seaweed. Replace the abalone in the shell on top of the seaweed and put into a steamer or on a rack above boiling water. Spoon the sake over each abalone, cover and steam for 20 minutes on moderate heat. Brush with miso sauce after about 12 minutes steaming. Remove the abalone, cut in half horizontally and then into 1.25cm/½ inch strips. Replace in the shells. Garnish with cucumber and ginger. Use any remaining miso sauce as a dipping sauce.

Steamed Chicken

PREPARATION TIME: 25 minutes

COOKING TIME: 15 minutes

SERVES: 4 people

450g/1lb chicken breasts, boned
10ml/2 tsps salt
30ml/2 tbsps sake
15ml/1 tbsp light soy sauce
15ml/1 tbsp dark soy sauce

4 leaves of Chinese cabbage
1 piece daikon radish
1 small red pepper

Prick the skin of the chicken and salt lightly. Mix the sake and soy sauce and pour over the chicken. Rub in well. Place chicken in a steamer or in a dish on a rack over boiling water. Cover and cook 15 minutes on moderate heat. Cut into 1.25cm/ ½ inch strips. Meanwhile, insert a vegetable peeler lengthwise into the daikon radish and remove a core.

Facing page: Beef Roasted with Vegetables.

Push in the pepper. Grate the two together, finely. Place the Chinese leaves/cabbage on plate and arrange the chicken. Garnish with small mounds of grated daikon radish. Reduce the cooking liquid from the chicken by boiling rapidly in a small saucepan. Use as a sauce.

Steamed Fish Rolls

PREPARATION TIME: 25 minutes

COOKING TIME: 10-15 minutes

SERVES: 4 people

*2 large sole or plaice/flounder to give
    4 whole fillets*
*4 spring/green onions, blanched
    2 minutes*
180g/6oz prawns/shrimp
10ml/2 tsps cornflour/cornstarch
5ml/1 tsp sake
2 eggs, beaten
Salt

GLAZE
15ml/1 tbsp white miso
15ml/1 tbsp mirin

GARNISH
*1 small piece pickled daikon radish,
    fanned*
4 whole prawns/shrimp

Skin the fish fillets and lay them skin side up on a flat surface. Chop the prawns/shrimp finely and mix with cornflour/cornstarch and sake. Divide the prawn/shrimp filling between the 2 fillets and spoon into a mound across the middle of the fillet. Trim off the white part of the onions and use only the green. Place the onions next to the prawn/shrimp filling. Cook the eggs with a pinch of salt until softly scrambled. Place in a mound next to the onions. Roll up the fish fillets, folding the thicker end over the filling first. Secure with cocktail sticks/wooden picks. Place in the top part of a steamer. Boil water in the bottom part. Alternatively, use a large pan and place the fish on a rack over boiling water. Steam for 10-15 minutes, until the fish is cooked. Five minutes before the end of cooking, brush with

combined glaze ingredients. Cut in slices and serve garnished with pickled daikon radish cut in a fan shape and whole prawns/shrimp.

Hakata-Mushi (Steamed Minced Pork)

PREPARATION TIME: 30 minutes

COOKING TIME: 50 minutes

SERVES: 4 people

*450g/1lb Chinese leaves/cabbage,
    parboiled 2 minutes*
3 eggs, beaten
450g/1lb minced/ground pork
30g/2 tbsps plain/all-purpose flour
15ml/1 tbsp soy sauce
Pinch salt

SAUCE
570ml/½ pint/2 cups dashi
45ml/3 tbsps soy sauce
½ clove garlic, finely minced
15ml/1 tbsp cornflour/cornstarch

Line the bottom of a greased 450g/ 1lb loaf pan with ⅓ of the cabbage leaves. Mix ⅓ of the beaten egg with the meat, flour, soy sauce and salt. Pour half of the remaining egg into the pan over the cabbage leaves. Press half of the meat mixture on top of the egg. Cover with another ⅓ of the cabbage leaves and add another layer of meat. Pour remaining egg over the meat and cover with remaining cabbage leaves. Press the mixture down and cover the pan with foil. Bring water to the boil in a steamer or large, deep pan with a tight-fitting lid. Place the pan in the steamer or on a rack above the water and cook 50 minutes, covered. Mix the cornflour/cornstarch with 30ml/ 2 tbsps of dashi. Bring the remaining dashi to the boil and add the soy sauce and garlic. Gradually stir in the cornflour/cornstarch and cook, stirring constantly until the mixture

Facing page: Steamed Chicken (top) and Hakata-Mushi (Steamed Minced Pork) (bottom). This page: Steamed Fish Rolls.

thickens. Cover the surface of the sauce with greaseproof/wax paper to prevent a skin forming. Allow the sauce to cool. Cool the hakata-mushi to room temperature and cut into squares or slices. Serve with the cooled sauce for dipping.

JAPANESE COOKING

SIMMERING AND ONE-POT COOKING

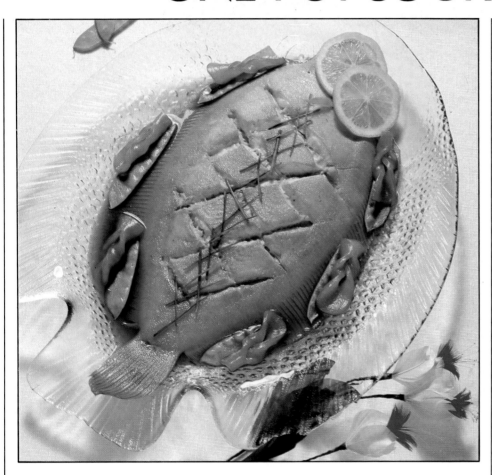

Simmered Flounder

PREPARATION TIME: 35 minutes

COOKING TIME: 27 minutes

SERVES: 4 people

140ml/¼ pint/½ cup sake
430ml/¾ pint/1½ cups dashi
140ml/¼ pint/½ cup mirin
140ml/¼ pint/½ cup soy sauce
4 small plaice/flounder or sole

120g/4oz mangetout/pea pods, steamed
* 2 minutes*
1 cake konnyaku

GARNISH
Lemon Slices
Shredded chives

Pour sake into a small saucepan and warm gently. Ignite the fumes and allow to burn until the flames die off naturally. Keep a pan lid handy in case the flames shoot up. Add the dashi, mirin and soy sauce. Gut the fish or buy already prepared. Leave on the heads and tails. Score the white side of the fish with a sharp knife. Put the fish cut sides down into a large, shallow pan. Pour over the stock and cook gently on top of the heat for 15-20 minutes. Remove the fish to serving dishes and turn cut side up. Keep warm. Cut the konnyaku cake into rectangles about 6mm/¼ inch thick. Cut a slit in the middle and pull the end of the konnyaku through the slit, twisting as you pull. Place in the fish cooking liquid and cook 5 minutes on gentle heat. Arrange the blanched mangetout/pea pods and konnyaku against the fish and spoon some of the cooking liquid over each.

Simmered Vegetables

PREPARATION TIME: 30 minutes

COOKING TIME: 7 minutes

SERVES: 4 people

900g/2lbs of a selection of the following:
Shiitake mushrooms, soaked 30 minutes,
* stalks removed*
Turnips, peeled and pared into thick
* barrel shapes*
Carrots, peeled

**This page: Simmered Flounder.
Facing page: Simmered Vegetables
(top) and Simmered Coltsfoot and
Carrots (bottom).**

Konnyaku cake, cut in 6mm/¼ inch
  slices
Courgettes/zucchini cut in 6mm/¼ inch
  diagonal slices
Mangetout/pea pods, strings removed if
  necessary, ends trimmed on the diagonal
Spring/green onions, cut in 2.5cm/1 inch
  diagonal pieces

BROTH
480ml/¾ pint/1½ cups dashi
10ml/2 tsps sake
60ml/4 tbsps soy sauce
45ml/3 tbsps mirin

Score the mushroom caps if desired.
Use a sharp, small knife to cut the
turnips into thick hexagonal shapes.
Take strips off the carrots, lengthwise,
with a cannelle knife or paring knife.
Cut crosswise into "flower" shapes.
Cut a lengthwise slit in the konnyaku
cake slices. Pull one end through the
slit, twisting as you pull. Bring the
dashi and sake to the boil in a
saucepan and add the turnip and
konnyaku. Blanch 1 minute. Remove
the vegetables and set aside. Put in
the mangetout/pea pods and
courgettes/zucchini. Blanch 30
seconds. Return the turnips and
konnyaku to the pan and add the
mushrooms and carrots. Add the
sugar, soy sauce and bring to the boil.
Allow to simmer 5 minutes. Add the
spring/green onions during the last
minute of cooking. Remove all the
vegetables with a draining spoon and
arrange in serving dishes. Allow the
sauce to boil rapidly to reduce it.
Add the mirin and cook 30 seconds.
Allow to cool slightly and pour over
the vegetables.

Chicken One Pot

PREPARATION TIME: 35 minutes

COOKING TIME: 30 minutes

SERVES: 6 people

30ml/2 tbsps oil
450g/1lb boned chicken, thinly sliced
280ml/½ pint/1 cup chicken stock
60ml/4 tbsp soy sauce
30ml/2 tbsps sugar
1 carrot, sliced diagonally
1 medium green pepper, cut in thin strips

225g/8oz fresh spinach leaves, well
  washed
8 shiitake mushrooms, soaked 30 minutes
1 piece tofu, sliced
1 small bunch coriander leaves
225g/8oz buckwheat noodles, cooked

SAUCE AND GARNISH
90ml/6 tbsps soy sauce
90ml/6 tbsps lemon juice
1 piece daikon radish, peeled and stuck
  with 1 small red chili pepper

Heat oil in an electric frying pan or
chafing dish at the table. Start frying
the chicken a few slices at a time. Mix
stock, soy sauce and sugar. When
chicken pieces are cooked, push to
the side of the pan and add some of
each vegetable and a small portion of
noodles. Moisten all with stock
mixture. Make a hole in the centre of
the daikon radish with a vegetable
peeler and push in the chili pepper.
Grate the two together finely and
serve in small mounds next to
mounds of onion. Serve the soy
sauce and lemon juice in individual
bowls. As the ingredients are cooked,
each person takes food from the pan.
A bit of the radish and onion may be
mixed into the dipping sauce. Dip
food into the sauce and continue to
cook ingredients as the meal goes on.

Simmered Chicken with Okra

PREPARATION TIME: 20 minutes

COOKING TIME: 12 minutes

SERVES: 4 people

430ml/¾ pint/1½ cups dashi or chicken
  stock
45ml/3 tbsps mirin
75ml/5 tbsps soy sauce
2 chicken breasts, boned and cut in slivers
140ml/½ pint/½ cup dashi or chicken
  stock
6 okra pods, stems trimmed and cut in
  rounds
1 piece tofu, cut in slices
Bamboo shoots cut in thin matchsticks

GARNISH
Carrot flowers (see introduction)

Prepare the garnish. Mix the first
3 ingredients and bring to the boil in
a shallow pan. Add the chicken and
cook 10 minutes on moderate heat.
Take off the heat and set aside. Add
remaining dashi to a small saucepan
with the okra, tofu and bamboo
shoots. Cook 2 minutes. Arrange the
chicken and vegetables in shallow
serving bowls. Pour over a small
amount of chicken cooking liquid.
Garnish with carrot flowers.

Simmered Coltsfoot and Carrots

PREPARATION TIME: 25 minutes

COOKING TIME: 14 minutes

SERVES: 4 people

2 coltsfoot stems (4 sticks celery may be
  substituted)
570ml/1 pint/2 cups dashi
15ml/1 tbsp sugar
30ml/2 tbsps mirin
30ml/2 tbsps soy sauce
1 small carrot, cut in thin ribbons
Bonito flakes

Cook the coltsfoot stems or celery
sticks whole in 1150ml/2 pints/
4 cups salted water. Cook 4 minutes.
Rinse under cold water. Peel the
stems from the bottom of the
coltsfoot and drain. Cut coltsfoot or
celery into 5cm/2 inch sticks.
Combine dashi, sugar, mirin and soy
sauce in a saucepan and bring to the
boil. Add the coltsfoot and simmer
10 minutes. Simmer only 5 minutes
for celery. Add the carrot ribbons
2 minutes before the end of cooking.
Remove the vegetables and arrange
in dishes. Allow the vegetables and
cooking liquid to cool. Pour some of
the liquid over each serving of
vegetables and serve cold, garnished
with bonito flakes.

**Facing page: Simmered Chicken
with Okra (top) and Chicken One
Pot (bottom).**

Simmered Prawns/Shrimp with Vegetables

PREPARATION TIME: 30 minutes

COOKING TIME: 2 minutes

SERVES: 4 people

225g/8oz prawns/shrimp or 450g/1lb
  king prawns/jumbo shrimp
2 medium carrots, peeled

This page: Sukiyaki. Facing page:
Cod and Cabbage One Pot (top)
and Simmered Prawns/Shrimp
with Vegetables (bottom).

16 French/green beans
1 small piece daikon radish, cut into
  matchsticks
1 piece kamaboku fish paste or konnyaku

60g/2oz bamboo shoots, cut into
  matchsticks
430ml/¾ pint/1½ cups dashi
15ml/1 tbsp mirin
1 small piece ginger, peeled and left whole

Cut strips from the carrot lengthwise
with a cannelle knife or paring knife.
Cut the carrot crosswise into 6mm/
¼ inch "flower" slices. Trim the ends
of the beans on the diagonal. Slice
the daikon pieces into thin
rectangles. Cut the kamaboku paste
into slices and cut a lengthwise slit in
the middle of each. Pull one end of
the paste through the slit, twisting
gently. Place the paste and all the
vegetables, except the mushrooms, in
a shallow pan and cover with water.
Add a pinch of salt and cover the
pan tightly. Cook about 2 minutes on
high heat, until the carrots are almost
tender. Add the bamboo shoots
halfway through cooking time.
Meanwhile, bring the dashi, mirin
and ginger to the boil in a shallow
pan. Leave the shells on the very
ends of the tails of the prawns/
shrimp. Place them in the hot dashi
and cook 2 minutes or until just pink.
Do not allow them to boil. Arrange
all the ingredients attractively in
4 shallow bowls. Spoon over some of
the dashi mixture and serve
immediately.

Sukiyaki

PREPARATION TIME: 40 minutes

COOKING TIME: 30 minutes

SERVES: 6 people

6 eggs, beaten
45ml/3 tbsps oil
675g/1½ lbs sirloin, sliced paper thin
1 bunch spring/green onions, cut in
  1.25cm/½ inch diagonal pieces
8 shiitake mushrooms, soaked 30 minutes
  and scored
140g/5oz shirataki noodles, soaked
  5 minutes and cut in 12cm/5 inch
  lengths
140g/5oz udon noodles, cooked
225g/8oz Chinese leaves/cabbage
225g/8oz fresh spinach, leaves washed
  and stems removed
2 bamboo shoots, cut in triangular pieces
1 150g/5oz cake konnyaku, sliced

1 150g/5oz cake tofu, sliced
Trefoil (salad cress) or watercress

BROTH
280ml/½ pint/1 cup dashi
140ml/¼ pint/½ cup soy sauce
45ml/3 tbsps mirin
15ml/1 tbsp sugar

Break one egg into each of 6 bowls and beat lightly. Arrange all the ingredients on a large tray. Heat oil in an electric frying pan or chafing dish at the table. Brown the meat a few pieces at a time. Add onions. Move meat to one side of the dish and add equal portions of the other ingredients. Mix broth ingredients together and add some to the pan. Each person takes some of the cooked food and dips it into the egg which quickly glazes the hot food. Keep adding ingredients and simmering liquid as the meal progresses.

Eternity Patties

PREPARATION TIME:	20 minutes
COOKING TIME:	13-15 minutes
SERVES:	4-5 people

340g/12oz minced/ground chicken
½ egg, beaten
30g/2 tbsps plain/all-purpose flour
2.5ml/½ tsp ground ginger
60g/2oz/½ cup plain/all-purpose flour
700ml/1¼ pints/2½ cups dashi
45ml/3 tbsps soy sauce
30ml/2 tbsps sugar
15ml/1 tbsp sake

GARNISH
Radish flowers and leaves

Combine the chicken, egg, 30g/ 2 tbsps flour, ginger and salt in a large bowl and mix well. Divide the mixture into 10 (mixture will be soft). Lightly flour hands and form mixture into patties. Coat the patties with the remaining flour mixed with a pinch of salt. Score a lattice on the top of each patty using the blunt side of a knife. Combine remaining ingredients in a large frying pan and bring to the boil. Add the patties to the pan,

scored side up, and swirl liquid over the tops. Reduce heat and simmer 3-4 minutes. Gently turn the patties over and cook 5-6 minutes. Turn again and increase the heat to bring the liquid up to a rapid boil. Quickly swirl the liquid over the patties for about 2 minutes. Transfer the patties to a serving dish and spoon over some of the cooking liquid. Garnish with radish flowers and leaves.

Cod and Cabbage One Pot

PREPARATION TIME:	40 minutes
COOKING TIME:	30 minutes
SERVES:	4 people

10 dried shiitake mushrooms, soaked
    30 minutes
450g/1lb cod fillet, skinned and cut in
    2.5cm/1 inch pieces
3 small leeks, washed and cut in 6cm/
    2½ inch lengths
225g/8oz Chinese leaves/cabbage
225g/8oz tofu, drained
45g/1½ oz cellophane noodles, soaked 5
    minutes
1.3 litres/2½ pints/5 cups dashi

SAUCE
30ml/2 tbsps rice vinegar
30ml/2 tbsps soy sauce
60ml/4 tbsps mirin
30ml/2 tbsps lemon juice
60ml/4 tbsps sake
1 small piece konbu seaweed

GARNISH
2 spring/green onions, finely chopped
90g/3oz piece daikon radish, stuck with
    1 red pepper, finely grated

Drain mushrooms and cut off stalks. Trim down spines of the cabbage leaves and cut the leaves into 3 irregular-shaped pieces. Cut the tofu into 10 pieces. Drain the noodles and arrange all the ingredients on a large tray. Bring the stock to the boil. Mix the sauce ingredients and pour into 4 small bowls. Arrange a mound of onion and one of grated daikon radish on 4 separate plates or trays. Put the pot of stock on an electric ring on the table. Add the fish, then

the mushrooms and then the cabbage leaves. Add the leeks, noodles and tofu. Each person mixes small amounts of onion and radish into the sauce and takes food from the main pot to dip into the sauce. A fondue pot may also be used for cooking.

Simmered Pork and Vegetable Casserole

PREPARATION TIME:	25 minutes
COOKING TIME:	1 hour
SERVES:	4 people

30ml/2 tbsps oil
450g/1lb pork spare ribs, cut in 2.5cm/
    1 inch pieces
30g/1oz piece ginger, sliced thinly
45ml/3 tbsps sake
60ml/4 tbsps soy sauce
30g/2 tbsps sugar
60g/2oz French/green beans, cut in
    5cm/2 inch lengths
2 sticks celery, cut in 5cm/2 inch lengths
60g/2oz bamboo shoots, cut into strips

Heat the oil in a large sauté pan. Cook the sliced ginger briefly and remove. Add the pork to the pan, turn up the heat and brown on all sides. Pour in water to just barely cover. Return the ginger to the pan. Add the sake, cover and cook for 1 hour. Check the level of liquid and add more water if the meat begins to dry out. When the pork is tender, add the soy sauce, sugar and cook, uncovered, to reduce the sauce to syrupy consistency. Meanwhile put beans and celery into a small pan and barely cover with water. Add a pinch of salt and bring to the boil. Cook 2-3 minutes until tender-crisp. Add the bamboo shoots after about 2 minutes. Place the pork in individual serving dishes and scatter over the vegetables. Pour over any remaining sauce.

Facing page: Simmered Pork and Vegetable Casserole (top) and Eternity Patties (bottom).

JAPANESE COOKING

DEEP-FRYING

Lemony Marinated Herring

PREPARATION TIME: 15 minutes

COOKING TIME: 10-20 minutes

SERVES: 4 people

4 herrings, cleaned and heads removed
45ml/3 tbsps rice vinegar
30ml/2 tbsps soy sauce
30ml/2 tbsps sake
15ml/1 tbsp lemon juice
Cornflour/cornstarch to dredge
Oil for frying

Score the fish diagonally 3 or 4 times on one side. Mix the vinegar, soy sauce, sake and lemon juice together and sprinkle over the fish. Leave in a cool place to marinate for 15 minutes. Heat oil to 350°F/180°C in a deep-fat fryer or wok. Dredge the fish with cornflour/cornstarch and fry in the hot oil, 2 fish at a time. Cook for 5-10 minutes. Drain on paper towels. Garnish with lemon and cucumber twigs, if desired.

Deep-Fried Pork

PREPARATION TIME: 15 minutes

COOKING TIME: 5 minutes per batch

SERVES: 4 people

4 slices pork loin or fillet/tenderloin,
*   about 1.25cm/½ inch thick*
Flour with salt and pepper
2 egg whites, lightly beaten
120g/4oz/1 cup fresh breadcrumbs
Oil for frying
½ head Chinese leaves/cabbage
1 lime, sliced

Clip the edges of the pork slices to prevent curling and dip in the

seasoned flour. Shake off excess flour and dip the pork into the egg white and then sprinkle with breadcrumbs. Heat the oil to 350°F/180°C in a deep-fat fryer or wok. Fry 1 or 2 slices

This page: Taksuta-Age (Deep-Fried Chicken) (top) and Deep-Fried Pork (bottom). Facing page: Snowy Fried Prawns/Shrimp (top) and Lemon Marinated Herring (bottom).

at a time for about 5 minutes. Remove the pork and drain on paper towels. Slice each piece diagonally into 1.25cm/½ inch thick strips. Serve assembled on a bed of shredded Chinese leaves/cabbage and garnish with lime slices.

Snowy Fried Prawns/ Shrimp

PREPARATION TIME: 20 minutes

COOKING TIME: 2 minutes per batch

SERVES: 4 people

675g/1½ lbs cooked king prawns/jumbo shrimp, peeled
60g/2oz harusame or saifan (soy flour noodles)
60g/2oz/½ cup flour with salt and pepper
2 egg whites
Oil for frying

De-vein the prawns/shrimp and score diagonally on the underside. Cut the noodles into 6mm-1.25cm/ ¼-½ inch pieces. Whisk the egg whites until foamy. Dip the prawns/shrimp into the seasoned flour and shake off surplus. Dip into egg white and then sprinkle on the noodles until each prawn/shrimp is completely covered. Heat oil in a deep-fat fryer or wok to 325°F/160°C. Add the prawns/ shrimp to the hot oil and fry a few at a time until the noodles look opaque, about 2 minutes. Drain well before serving. They should not be allowed to brown.

Vegetable Tempura

PREPARATION TIME: 30 minutes

COOKING TIME: 2 minutes per batch

SERVES: 4 people

Selection of the following ingredients prepared as directed:
Celery, cut into sticks
Artichoke hearts, halved
Lotus root, sliced in rounds about 6mm/ ¼ inch thick
Mushrooms, whole fresh or dried, soaked 30 minutes, with stems removed

Green peppers, cut in 6mm/¼ inch thick rings or strips
Onions, cut in 6mm/¼ inch rings
Parsnips, peeled and cut into sticks
Asparagus tips
Turnips, peeled and cubed
Mangetout/pea pods, ends trimmed and strings removed if necessary
French beans/green beans, ends trimmed
Aubergine/eggplant, cut in half. Cut away flesh, leaving 3mm/⅛ inch clinging to the skin. Cut the skin into fan shapes about 3.75cm/1½ inches long
Courgettes/zucchini, cut in half lengthwise and then into thin slices across
Okra, stems removed and pods left whole
Broccoli, cut into flowerets
Cauliflower, cut into flowerets
Parsley, snipped into small bunches
Sweet potato, peeled and sliced into 1.25cm/½ inch rounds
Carrots, peeled and cut into diagonal slices
Cucumber, cut in quarters lengthwise and then into 2.5cm/1 inch wedges
Oil for frying

DIPPING SAUCE
120ml/4 fl oz/½ cups chicken stock
60ml/4 tbsps soy sauce
60ml/4 tbsps sherry or sake
Pinch sugar
Small piece daikon radish, grated
Small piece ginger, grated

BATTER
1 egg yolk
280ml/½ pint/1¼ cups iced water
120g/4 oz/1 cup plain/all-purpose flour

Prepare the vegetables as directed. Mix all the ingredients for the sauce except the radish and ginger. Pour the sauce into 4 small bowls. Place a small mound of grated radish and one of grated ginger on each of 4 plates. Heat oil in a deep-fat fryer to 350°F/180°C. A wok may also be used. Beat the egg yolk lightly and beat in the water. Sift in the flour and stir with a table knife. The batter should look lumpy and under-mixed. Dip each vegetable in the batter and shake off the excess. Lower ingredients carefully into the hot oil and cook for about 2 minutes, turning once or twice with a metal spoon. Fry only 3 or 4 pieces at a

time and fry only 1 kind of vegetable at a time. Do not coat too many vegetables in advance. Drain fried vegetables on paper towels on a rack for a few seconds before serving. Serve while still hot and crisp. Each person may mix a desired amount of the grated radish and ginger into the dipping sauce to eat with the tempura.

Taksuta-Age (Deep-Fried Chicken)

PREPARATION TIME: 15 minutes, plus marinating time

COOKING TIME: 2-3 minutes per batch

SERVES: 4 people

4 chicken breasts
45ml/3 tbsps soy sauce
15ml/1 tbsp mirin or sweet sherry
15ml/1 tbsp rice vinegar
10ml/2 tbps sugar
1 clove garlic, minced
60g/2oz flour, with a pinch of salt and pepper
Oil for frying

Cut the chicken into 2.5cm/1 inch cubes and combine with all remaining ingredients except flour in a deep bowl and leave to marinate, covered, for about 1 hour in a cool place. Stir occasionally to coat the chicken evenly. Remove the chicken from the marinade with a draining spoon. Toss in the seasoned flour to coat. Heat the oil in a deep-fat fryer or wok to 350°F/180°C and fry the chicken, a few pieces at a time. Cook until golden brown and crisp, about 2-3 minutes per batch. Drain on paper towels a few seconds before serving. Serve with extra soy sauce for dipping, if desired.

Facing page: Vegetable Tempura.

Fish Tempura

| **PREPARATION TIME:** 30 minutes |
| **COOKING TIME:** 2 minutes per batch |
| **SERVES:** 4 people |

12 uncooked king prawns/jumbo shrimp
2 whitefish fillets, skinned and cut into
  5 x 2cm/2 x ¾ inch strips
Small whole fish such as smelt or
  whitebait
Squid, cleaned and cut into strips
  2.5 x 7.5cm/1 x 3 inches and dredged
  with flour
Oil for frying

DIPPING SAUCE
90ml/3 fl oz/⅓ cup soy sauce
Juice and zest of 1 lemon or lime
60ml/2 fl oz/¼ cup dashi

BATTER
1 egg yolk
240ml/8 fl oz/1 cup iced water
120g/4oz/1 cup plain/all-purpose flour,
  sifted

Shell the prawns/shrimp, leaving
only the tail shell on the end of each.
De-vein if necessary. Wash the whole
fish and pat dry. Prepare other fish as
directed. Mix the dipping sauce

ingredients and pour into small
bowls. Heat oil in a deep-fat fryer to
350°F/180°C. A wok may also be
used. To make the batter, beat the egg
yolk lightly and gradually beat in the
iced water. Sift in the flour and stir
the batter with a table knife. Batter
will be lumpy and look under-mixed.
Dip each piece of fish in the batter
and shake off the excess. Lower
ingredients carefully into the hot oil
and cook for about 2 minutes,
turning once or twice with a metal
spoon. Fry only 3 or 4 pieces of fish
at a time, and only 1 kind of fish at a
time. Do not coat too many pieces of

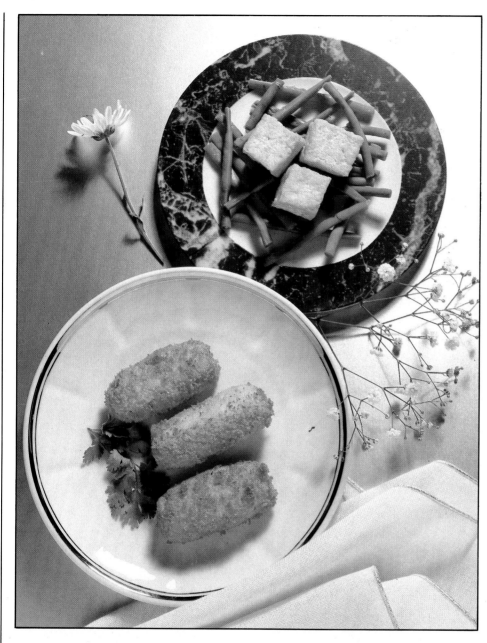

1 inch cubes. Heat the oil in a deep-fat fryer or wok to 350°F/180°C. Reduce heat slightly and add the tofu cubes to the hot oil. Deep-fry 1-2 minutes or until cubes float to the surface. Turn them over and fry a further 1 minute. Remove from the oil with a draining spoon and drain on a rack or paper towels. Cook tofu in several batches. Meanwhile, bring the stock to the boil in a saucepan. Add the beans and bonito flakes and simmer gently for 5 minutes until the beans are just tender. Transfer the beans to a serving dish with a draining spoon. Arrange them in a circle and keep warm. Rapidly boil the cooking liquid to reduce by half and pour over the beans. Pile the deep-fried tofu into the centre of the beans to serve.

Chicken Croquettes

PREPARATION TIME: 20 minutes

COOKING TIME: 3-5 minutes per batch

SERVES: 4 people

225g/8oz minced/ground chicken
225g/8oz cooked, mashed potatoes
½ small onion, finely chopped
1 clove garlic, minced
30ml/2 tbsps chopped parsley
Salt
Pepper
15ml/1tbsp soy sauce
1 egg, beaten
225g/8oz/1 cup breadcrumbs
Oil for frying

Combine the chicken, potatoes, onion, garlic, parsley, salt, pepper and soy sauce together in a mixing bowl. Add the egg and mix well. Form the mixture into small cylinder shapes about 5 x1.25cm/2 x ½ inch. Roll in breadcrumbs and chill briefly. Heat oil to 350°F/180°C in a deep-fat fryer or wok. Lower the croquettes carefully into the hot oil and fry for about 3-5 minutes, until golden brown and crisp. Cook in small batches. Drain on paper towels on a rack for a few seconds before serving. Serve with soy sauce for dipping if desired.

fish in advance. Drain on a rack with paper towels for a few seconds before serving. Serve while still hot and crisp with the sauce for dipping.

Deep-Fried Tofu with Green Beans

PREPARATION TIME: 20 minutes

COOKING TIME: 5 minutes for beans, 1-2 minutes per batch for tofu

SERVES: 4 people

Facing page: Fish Tempura. This page: Deep-Fried Tofu with Green Beans (top) and Chicken Croquettes (bottom).

450g/1lb tofu
240ml/8 fl oz/1 cup chicken stock
225g/8oz French/green beans, trimmed
15ml/1tbsp bonito flakes
Oil for frying

Drain and press tofu to remove excess moisture and cut into 2.5 cm/

JAPANESE COOKING

VINEGARED FOOD AND SALADS

Spinach and Bean Sprouts with Wasabi

PREPARATION TIME: 15 minutes

COOKING TIME: 1 minutes

SERVES: 4 people

1lb fresh spinach, washed well and stalks
    removed
4oz bean sprouts

DRESSING
2 tbsps rice vinegar
2 tbsps sugar
1 tbsp soy sauce
½ tsp wasabi powder mixed to a paste
    with water

Cook the spinach 1 minute in a
covered saucepan with only the
water that clings to the leaves after
washing. Refresh under cold water,
press to remove excess moisture and
leave to drain. Combine leaves with
bean sprouts. Mix dressing ingredients
very well and pour over salad. Toss
lightly and serve in individual bowls.

Daikon and Carrot Salad

PREPARATION TIME: 25 minutes

SERVES: 4 people

4 small oranges
½ daikon radish, peeled and coarsely
    grated
1 large carrot, peeled and coarsely grated
1 small piece ginger, grated
Rice vinegar
2 tbsps sugar
Pinch salt

GARNISH
Radish flowers and leaves

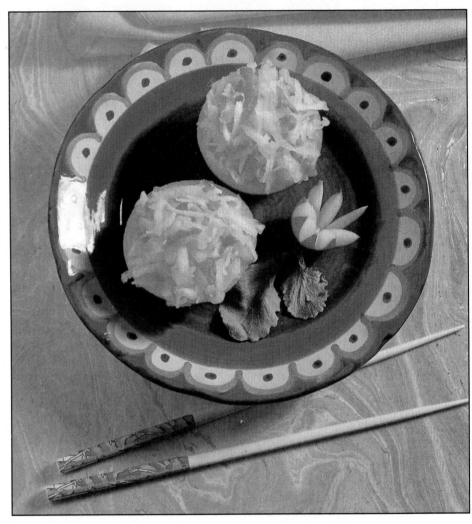

Cut the oranges in half and squeeze
for juice. Measure the juice and add
an equal amount of vinegar. Add the
sugar and salt and mix well. Cook
over low heat to dissolve sugar and
evaporate vinegar fumes. Set the
dressing aside to cool. Cut a slice
from the rounded end of the orange
shells so that they stand level. Do
not cut completely through the base.
Scoop out the orange pulp and cut

**This page: Daikon and Carrot
Salad. Facing page: Bean Salad
with Sesame Dressing (top) and
Spinach and Bean Sprouts with
Wasabi (bottom).**

the edge in scallops or points if
desired. Mix radish, carrot and ginger
with the dressing. Leave to stand 30
minutes. Fill orange shells with the
salad and serve chilled.

Gold Salad

PREPARATION TIME: 20 minutes

COOKING TIME: 6-8 minutes

SERVES: 4 people

20 spears white asparagus, stalks trimmed
Salt

SAUCE
2 egg yolks
30ml/2 tbsps rice vinegar
10ml/2 tsps dry mustard
15ml/1 tbsp sugar
10ml/2 tsps cornflour/cornstarch
60ml/4 tbsps dashi
Chopped parsley

Cut the asparagus into 5cm/2 inch diagonal pieces, leaving the tips whole. Bring 570ml/1 pint/2 cups water to the boil. Add a pinch of salt and the asparagus. Cook 2-3 minutes. Asparagus should still be crisp. Rinse in cold water and drain.

Combine all ingredients for the sauce in a double boiler or in a small bowl in a bain marie. Stirring constantly, cook over boiling water to thicken. Remove and stir or wisk until the sauce cools. It should be the consistency of mayonnaise. Divide asparagus into 4 bowls, spoon over the sauce and sprinkle on chopped parsley.

GARNISH
3 spring/green onions, very finely chopped

Pre-heat a grill/broiler, or cook over charcoal. Dry mushrooms well. Cut stalks off and sprinkle caps with salt. Cut the tofu into 1.25cm/½ inch slices. Brush lightly with oil on both sides. Grill/broil with the mushrooms, about 3 minutes per side, turning once. Cut mushrooms and tofu into thin slices. Arrange on dishes and mix the sauce ingredients. Pour over the mushrooms and tofu. Garnish with the onion. Serve hot.

Okra with Garlic and Seven Spice Pepper

PREPARATION TIME: 15 minutes

COOKING TIME: 5 minutes

SERVES: 4 people

40 okra pods
15ml/1 tbsp soy sauce
2 cloves garlic, grated finely
Seven spice pepper

Wash the okra well. Keep stem end on and put okra into boiling, salted water. Cook 5 minutes. Refresh under cold water and drain well. Cut off the stem ends. If the pods are small, leave whole. If large cut on the diagonal into 1.25cm/½ inch lengths. Sprinkle over soy sauce, garlic and pepper. Toss and serve in small bowls.

Broad Beans in Tofu Dressing

PREPARATION TIME: 25 minutes

COOKING TIME: 5 minutes

SERVES: 4 people

900g/2lbs fresh broad/lima beans
(weight when shelled)
Salt

DRESSING
1 225g/8oz cake tofu
30ml/2 tbsps sugar
Pinch salt
10ml/2 tsps sesame oil
2.5ml/½ tsp soy sauce

Facing page: Okra with Garlic and Seven Spice Pepper (top) and Broad Beans in Tofu Dressing (bottom). This page: Gold Salad (top) and Vinegared Mushroom Salad with Tofu (bottom).

Vinegared Mushroom Salad with Tofu

PREPARATION TIME: 30 minutes

COOKING TIME: 3 minutes

SERVES: 4 people

12 large shiitake mushrooms, soaked
30 minutes
1 225g/8oz cake tofu, drained
Salt
Oil

SAUCE
45ml/3 tbsps lemon juice
45ml/3 tbsps rice vinegar
90ml/6 tbsps soy sauce
Dash mirin

45ml/3 tbsps hot water
Black sesame seeds

Cook the beans in lots of boiling, salted water for about 5 minutes. Reserve the water. Rinse beans in cold water and peel off their outer skins, using only the bright green inner beans. Lower the cake of tofu carefully into the boiling water left from the beans. Leave tofu in the water about 5 seconds and remove with a draining spoon. Drain well and wrap in muslin/cheesecloth and press gently to extract all moisture. Blend in a food processor or blender with remaining dressing ingredients except sesame seeds. Pour over beans and sprinkle on sesame seeds.

Vinegared Crab

PREPARATION TIME: 25 minutes

COOKING TIME: 3 minutes

SERVES: 4 people

1 small cucumber, grated
1 large cooked crab
1 small piece ginger, grated

SAUCE
30ml/2 tbsps rice vinegar
30ml/2 tbsps dashi
60ml/4 tbsps mirin
15ml/1 tbsps soy sauce

GARNISH
Chinese leaves/cabbage
Grated pickled ginger

Sprinkle cucumber with salt and leave to stand 30 minutes. Bring sauce ingredients to the boil and set aside to cool. Pour into small bowls. Rinse and drain the cucumber. Press to remove excess moisture. Crack legs and claws off the crab. Remove the meat from the claws and leave the thin legs whole. Separate the underbody from the shell and remove the stomach sac and gills and discard. Scrape all the brown meat from the shell and crack the body into 4 pieces. Use a skewer to pick out the meat. Combine all meat with the ginger and cucumber and toss carefully. Arrange Chinese leaves/cabbage on plates or trays and pile

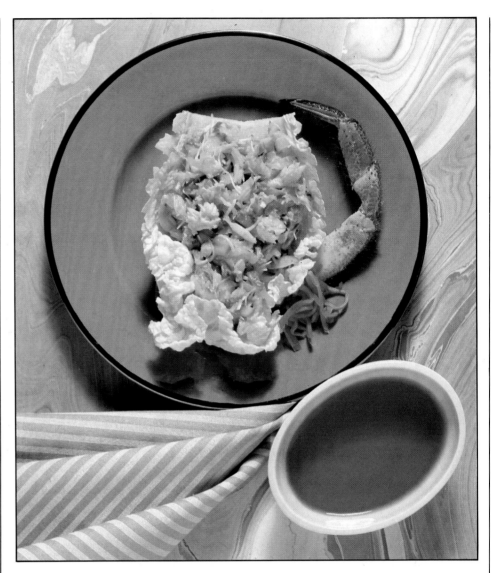

This page: Vinegared Crab. Facing page: Sushi.

salad on, leaving some of the leaves showing on each plate. Garnish with whole crab legs and pickled ginger. Serve the sauce for dipping.

Bean Salad with Sesame Dressing

PREPARATION TIME: 15 minutes

COOKING TIME: 2 minutes

SERVES: 4 people

225g/8oz French/green beans, trimmed
*   and cut in 5cm/2 inch lengths*
Salt

DRESSING
30ml/2 tbsps sesame paste
15ml/1 tbsp sugar
10ml/2 tsps soy sauce
10ml/2 tsps rice vinegar
Black sesame seeds

Bring water to the boil in a large pan with a pinch of salt. Add the beans and cook for 2 minutes after the water comes back to the boil. Drain and refresh under cold water. Leave to drain and dry. Mix all ingredients for the dressing except sesame seeds. Spoon over the beans and toss lightly. Sprinkle on seeds and serve in individual bowls.

JAPANESE COOKING

RICE, NOODLES AND PICKLES

Sushi

PREPARATION TIME: 40 minutes

COOKING TIME: 18 minutes

SERVES: 6-8 people

RICE
600g/1¼ lbs/2½ cups short grain rice
Small piece konbu seaweed
1 litre/1¾ pints/3½ cups water
5ml/1 tbsp sake

ROLLED SUSHI
4 sheets nori
½ cucumber
2 pieces pickled red ginger
Wasabi horseradish

LAYERED SUSHI
2 sheets nori
½ cucumber
120g/4oz smoked salmon, thinly sliced

SWEET VINEGAR
120ml/8 tbsps rice vinegar
50ml/3 tbsps sugar
Pinch salt

Rinse raw rice until water is almost clear. Leave in a colander 1 hour to drain. Meanwhile toast sheets of nori over a gas flame for 1 minute to freshen. Mix wasabi with enough water to make a paste. Slice the cucumber in half lengthwise. Reserve one half and quarter the other half. Mix the sweet vinegar ingredients and heat slowly in a small saucepan until sugar is dissolved. Leave to cool completely. Bring the water to the boil in a large pan with the piece of konbu. Remove the seaweed as soon as the water reaches a rolling boil. Add the sake and rice. Bring back to the boil and cook for 30 seconds on high heat. Lower the heat and cook for a further 12 minutes, covered.

Turn up the heat again and cook for 5 minutes to evaporate excess moisture. Take the pan off the heat and leave to stand, covered, for 10-15 minutes. Transfer the hot rice to a clean bowl and toss with the sweet vinegar. Cover the bowl with a damp towel until ready to use. Place 1 sheet of nori on a clean towel or piece of greaseproof/wax paper. If you have

Japanese bamboo mats these are ideal to use. Divide rice mixture in half and reserve half, covered. Divide half the mixture in fourths and spread some on the sheet of nori across the end closest to you. Spread some of the wasabi carefully over the rice. Cut a quarter of the cucumber to fit the sheet of nori and place on top of the rice. Cover the cucumber with another layer of rice and press it around firmly. Fold the end of the nori over the rice and tuck in the sides. Roll up using the towel, paper or mat to help you. Roll tightly, tucking in the sides as you roll. Repeat with the remaining rice, the remaining quarter of cucumber and use the same method with the pickled ginger, leaving out the wasabi. Leave each roll to stand, seam side down, for at least 2 minutes before slicing into 4-6 pieces with a dampened knife.

To make the layered sushi, line 2 15 or 20cm/6 or 8 inch oblong pans with clingfilm/plastic wrap. Divide the remaining rice mixture in half. Press half of that into one of the pans. Place the nori on top of the rice and cover with another layer of rice. Slice the cucumber lengthwise into thin slices. Place on top of the rice. Cover with another sheet of clingfilm/plastic wrap and place another pan of the same size on top. Press down and weight lightly. Leave to stand 5-10 minutes before removing form the pan and slicing the sushi into 5cm/2 inch pieces. Use the same method with the remaining rice and top with smoked salmon. Arrange the rolled and layered sushi on a large serving plate and give each person a bowl of soy sauce for dipping if desired.

Chrysanthemum Rice

PREPARATION TIME: 30 minutes

COOKING TIME: 30 minutes

MAKES: 15 balls

225g/8oz/1 cup short grain rice
300ml/10 fl oz/1¼ cups water
45ml/3 tbsps soy sauce
½ sheet nori
15ml/1 tbsp toasted sesame seeds
1 piece ginger, grated
6 eggs
45ml/3 tbsps dashi
15ml/1 tbsp sugar
15ml/1 tbsp sherry or sake
Oil for frying
Red caviar to garnish

Cook rice as for Chicken Donbun. Sprinkle soy sauce over warm rice, toss and cover with a damp cloth. Pre-heat oven to 250°F/130°C, place a sheet of nori on a baking tray and let dry for 3-4 minutes. When dry, crumble the nori. Add to the rice with the toasted sesame seeds and ginger, and toss lightly. With dampened hands, divide rice into 15 balls. Place 1 ball in the centre of a piece of muslin/cheesecloth, gather up the ends and twist cloth to form a firm ball of rice. Remove rice ball from the cloth and repeat with all the remaining rice. Dampen fingers and flatten the rice balls slightly. Cover with a damp cloth and set aside. Combine eggs, dashi, sugar and

This page: Sekihan (Red Rice) (top) and Chicken Donbun (bottom). **Facing page:** Chrysanthemum Rice (top) and Onigiri (bottom).

sherry or sake in a bowl and beat well. Lightly oil a 6 inch omelette pan or frying pan and heat. Add about 60ml/4 tbsps of the egg mixture to the pan and cook over medium heat for 1½ minutes, until edges are dry. Turn omelette over and continue cooking until set, about 30 seconds-1 minute. Transfer to a plate and repeat with remaining egg mixture. Let cool completely and then cut into thin

strips, about 7.5-10cm/3-4 inch long. Lay the omelette strips over each rice ball to form "chrysanthemum petals." Make a slight indentation in the middle of each one and fill with a little red caviar.

Chicken Donbun

| PREPARATION TIME: 15 minutes |
| COOKING TIME: 40 minutes |
| SERVES: 4 people |

225g/8oz cooked chicken
225g/8oz/1 cup short grain rice
430ml/¾ pint/1½ cups water
240ml/8 fl oz/1 cup chicken stock
30ml/2 tbsps sweet sherry or mirin
30ml/2 tbsps soy sauce
225g/8oz fresh mushrooms, sliced
120g/4oz peas
3 eggs
5ml/1 tsp salt

Cut the chicken into bite-sized pieces and set aside. Rinse the rice under cold water until the water runs almost clear. Leave in a colander to drain. Put the rice and water into a heavy-based saucepan and bring to the boil. Reduce the heat and simmer, covered, for 15 minutes until the rice is tender and the water is just absorbed. Stir and leave to stand, covered for 10-15 minutes before using. Put the stock, sherry, soy sauce, mushrooms and peas into a saucepan and bring to the boil. Reduce heat and simmer for 1-2 minutes until vegetables are tender. Add the rice and chicken and stir gently. Beat the egg and salt together and add to the ingredients in the saucepan. Cook over low heat, stirring occasionally until egg is just set. Serve immediately.

Sekihan (Red Rice)

| PREPARATION TIME: 15 minutes plus soaking time |
| COOKING TIME: 55-57 minutes |
| SERVES: 4 people |

60g/2oz/¼ cup azuki beans (small red beans), soaked overnight

300g/10oz/1½ cups short grain rice
30ml/2 tbsps black sesame seeds

Rinse beans and place in a saucepan with 570ml/1 pint/2 cups water. Bring to the boil and then simmer, uncovered, for 10-12 minutes or until beans begin to soften. Drain and reserve the cooking liquid. Wash the rice until the water runs almost clear. Soak the rice in half the bean liquid for about 2 hours. Reserve remaining bean liquid. Drain the rice and mix with beans. Spread both out on a plate in an even layer. Place the plate in the top part of a steamer or on a rack above boiling water. Cover tightly and steam 15 minutes. Uncover and spoon over about ⅓ of the remaining bean liquid. Re-cover and steam a further 10 minutes. Repeat the procedure twice more during cooking. Rice and beans should steam about 45 minutes. Toss the red rice to fluff it up and sprinkle over sesame seeds to serve.

Garnished Noodles

| PREPARATION TIME: 25 minutes |
| COOKING TIME: 20 minutes |
| SERVES: 4 people |

SAUCE
45ml/3 tbsps white wine vinegar
45ml/3 tbsps soy sauce
10ml/2 tsps sugar
140ml/¼ pint/½ cup chicken stock or dashi
450g/1lb soba noodles
1150ml/2 pints/4 cups water

GARNISHES
Cucumber, diced
120g/4oz small, cooked and peeled shrimp
Celery leaves
2 sheets nori, toasted and crumbled or shredded

Combine vinegar, soy sauce, stock/dashi in a saucepan and bring to the boil. Remove from the heat and keep warm. Bring water to the boil and add the noodles. Stir once and bring back to the boil. Simmer gently until tender, about 5 minutes. Drain in a colander and rinse with hot water.

Divide the noodles among 4 serving dishes and arrange garnishes on top. Pour over the sauce and serve.

Five-Coloured Noodles

| PREPARATION TIME: 25 minutes |
| COOKING TIME: 18-20 minutes |
| SERVES: 4 people |

225g/8oz ubon or somen noodles
1150ml/2 pints/4 cups water
140ml/¼ pint/½ cup chicken stock
1 carrot cut into diagonal slices
1 small turnip, diced
4 dried shiitake mushrooms, soaked 30 minutes, drained and stalks removed, and sliced
120g/4oz French/green beans, cut into 3.75cm/1½ inch strips
10ml/2 tsps cornflour/cornstarch
45ml/3 tbsps soy sauce
20ml/4 tsps black sesame seeds

Cook noodles as for Garnished Noodles. Rinse under cold water and drain thoroughly. In a saucepan, bring the stock to the boil; add carrot, turnip, mushrooms and beans and cover the pan. Simmer 8-10 minutes until just tender. Blend cornflour/cornstarch and soy sauce together and add to the stock. Continue cooking until slightly thickened. Divide the noodles among 4 serving bowls and pour over the vegetables. Sprinkle with black sesame seeds and serve.

Onigiri

| PREPARATION TIME: 30 minutes |
| COOKING TIME: 25 minutes |
| SERVES: 6 people |

450g/1lb short grain rice
700ml/1¼ pints/2½ cups water
60ml/4 tbsps black sesame seeds
Seven spice pepper
2 sheets nori

Facing page: Five-Coloured Noodles (top) and Garnished Noodles (bottom).

Cook rice as for Chicken Donbun. Dampen hands with salt water and shape hot rice into cakes, triangles and oblongs. Rice moulds are available in various shapes and may be used instead of the hand-shaping method. Place the moulds on a flat surface and fill with rice. Use the pusher to press the rice firmly into shape and then remove the mould. Toast the nori sheets over a gas flame and cut into strips. Wrap a strip around each rice oblong. Decorate one of the other shapes with black sesame seeds and the other with the seven spice pepper. Serve warm. In Japan, these are often eaten as snacks.

Cauliflower and Broccoli Pickles

PREPARATION TIME: 20 minutes

COOKING TIME: 3 minutes

SERVES: 4 people

1 small head cauliflower, cut in flowerets
120g/4oz broccoli, cut in flowerets

DRESSING
15ml/1 tbsp wasabi horseradish
90ml/6 tbsps soy sauce
30ml/2 tbsps mirin
Black sesame seeds

Bring lots of salted water to the boil in a large saucepan and add the prepared vegetables. Mix the remaining ingredients and set aside. Cook vegetables about 3 minutes. Drain and refresh under cold water. Leave to dry. Toss with the dressing and refrigerate 3 hours before serving.

Cucumber Pickles

PREPARATION TIME: 30 minutes

SERVES: 4 people

10ml/2 tsps sesame seeds, mixed with
   15ml/1 tbsp oil
1 cucumber
30-60ml/2-4 tbsps soy sauce
Bonito flakes

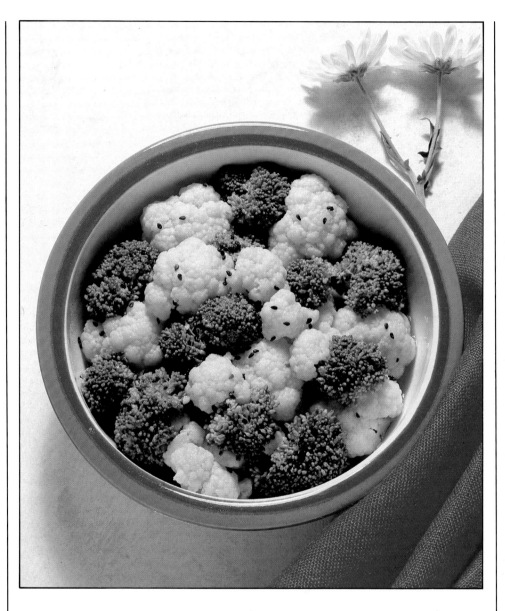

Spread the sesame seeds over the bottom of a heavy frying pan and cook over gentle heat until lightly browned. Peel the cucumbers and cut into 2.5cm/1 inch irregular wedges. Combine all ingredients except the bonito flakes and leave to marinate 20 minutes in a cool place. Sprinkle bonito flakes on top before serving.

Lemon Turnips

PREPARATION TIME: 20 minutes plus chilling time

SERVES: 4 people

4 medium turnips
Juice and rind of ½ lemon

This page: Cauliflower and Broccoli Pickles. Facing page: Lemon Turnips (top) and Cucumber Pickles (bottom).

Salt
1 small piece nori, shredded

Peel turnips and cut into large dice. Combine all the ingredients except nori. Put into a large bowl. Press a smaller bowl on top and weight. Refrigerate overnight. When ready to serve, refresh nori over a gas flame and shred finely. Sprinkle over the top of the pickle.

DESSERTS

sugar until dissolved. Sprinkle on the agar-agar and whisk until dissolved. Dampen an 1150ml/2 pint/4 cup loaf pan and pour in the mixture. Leave in the refrigerator to set. Unmould onto a serving dish. Slice the kiwi fruit and arrange on top of the jelly.

Sweet Tempura

PREPARATION TIME: 20 minutes

COOKING TIME: 2-3 minutes per batch

SERVES: 4 people

Selection of the following prepared as
    directed:
Strawberries, hulled, washed and drained
Kiwi fruit, peeled and cut into 6mm/
    ¼ inch slices
Apples, cored and cut into wedges, lightly
    sprinkled with lemon juice
Pears, peeled, cored and cut into wedges,
    lightly sprinkled with lemon juice
Pineapple, peeled, cored and cut in rings
    or pieces
Banana, peeled and sliced, lightly
    sprinkled with lemon juice
Plums, small ones left whole
Tangerine, peeled and segmented
Melon, peeled, seeded and cut into cubes
    or wedges

BATTER
1 egg
140ml/¼ pint/½ cup water
90g/3oz/¾ cup plain/all-purpose flour
60g/2oz/¼ cup cornflour/cornstarch

Clear honey

Orange and Kiwi Jelly

PREPARATION TIME: 20 minutes

SERVES: 4-6 people

430ml/¾ Pint/1½ cups orange juice
140ml/¼ pint/½ cup water

120g/4oz/½ cup sugar
10ml/2 tsps agar-agar
1 or 2 kiwi fruit, peeled

Put orange juice and water into a saucepan and heat until boiling. Remove from the heat and stir in the

This page: Sweet Tempura. Facing page: Orange and Kiwi Jelly.

Prepare fruit before preparing the batter. Pre-heat oil in a deep-fat fryer or wok to 350°F/180°C. Lightly beat egg and stir in the water. Sift in the flour and cornflour/cornstarch and stir in with a table knife. Do not overmix; batter should be lumpy. Dip the fruit into the batter and lower carefully into the hot oil. Cook for 2-3 minutes until lightly golden and crisp. Cook in small batches and cook only one kind of fruit at a time. Drain a few seconds on paper towels. Arrange on serving plates and drizzle with honey. Serve immediately.

Nishiki-Tamago (Brocade Eggs)

PREPARATION TIME: 15 minutes

COOKING TIME: 20 minutes

OVEN TEMPERATURE: 325°F/ 150°C/Gas Mark 3

10 eggs
200g/7oz/scant 1 cup sugar
Pinch salt

Bring a large saucepan of water to the boil. Carefully lower in the eggs and bring back to the boil. Cook the eggs 10 minutes from the time the water begins to boil. Run cold water over the eggs until they are completely cooled. If prepared in advance, leave in shells in cold water. To prepare, peel eggs and push the whites and yolks through a metal strainer, keeping them separate. Egg whites can be finely chopped in a food processor. Mix the whites with a pinch of salt and about 90g/3oz/⅓ cup of the sugar. Mix the egg yolks with remaining sugar. Place the whites in a square pan and press down lightly. Cover with the yolk mixture and press again. Bake for 10 minutes. Allow to cool completely and cut into 2.5-5cm/1-2 inch pieces.

Sweet Potato and Chestnut Pudding

PREPARATION TIME: 30 minutes

COOKING TIME: 30 minutes

SERVES: 6-8 people

300g/10oz sweet potatoes, peeled and sliced
120g/4oz can whole chestnuts in syrup
45ml/3 tbsps sugar
30ml/2 tbsps mirin or sherry
15ml/1 tbsp cornflour/cornstarch
60ml/4 tbsps water

Soak sweet potatoes in cold water for 30 minutes. Place in fresh water in a large saucepan. Cover and bring to the boil. Cook about 20 minutes, or until very soft. Drain and dry over low heat, mashing with a fork or potato masher until smooth. Meanwhile drain the chestnuts and reserve the syrup. Mix syrup with sugar and bring slowly to the boil in a heavy-based pan. Cook until the sugar dissolves and mixture thickens slightly. Mix half the syrup with the sweet potatoes. Cook the potatoes again over moderate heat, beating constantly with a wooden spoon until the potatoes thicken. Chop half the chestnuts roughly and add to the potatoes. Mound the pudding into a serving dish and decorate with whole chestnuts. Mix the remaining syrup with the mirin and the cornflour/

cornstarch dissolved in the water. Bring syrup to the boil. Stir and cook until thickened. Allow to cool completely and pour over the pudding to serve.

Almond Sesame Cookies

PREPARATION TIME: 15 minutes

COOKING TIME: 10-20 minutes

OVEN TEMPERATURE: 325°F/ 150°C/Gas Mark 3

MAKES: 20

30ml/2 tbsps sesame oil
120ml/4 fl oz/½ cup water
120g/4oz/1 cup raisins
225g/8oz/1 cup sesame seeds
1 egg, beaten
Few drops almond essence/extract
120g/4oz/½ cup sugar
120g/4oz/1 cup self-raising flour or
    plain/all-purpose flour and 5ml/1 tsp
    baking powder
120g/4oz/1 cup whole-wheat flour
20 whole almonds

Pre-heat oven. Place the sesame oil, water, raisins, sesame seeds, egg and almond essence/extract in a bowl

Facing page: Nishiki-Tamago (Brocade Eggs) (top) and Almond Sesame Cookies (bottom). This page: Sweet Potato and Chestnut Pudding.

and mix well. Sift in sugar, the flours and baking powder, if using and mix to a stiff dough. Divide the mixture into 20 portions and roll each into a ball. Arrange the balls on a greased baking sheet and press an almond into the top of each, flattening them slightly. Bake 10 minutes depending on the number of cookies. The cookies should be crisp and golden when done.

JAPANESE COOKING